921983 $8.95
j220.950 Haan, Sheri Dunham.
HAA   God speaks to
           king

W9-ATQ-970

CHILDREN'S DEPARTMENT
THE BRUMBACK LIBRARY

BRUMBACK LIBRARY
God speaks to a king :
Haan, Sheri Dunham.   220.950 HAA
JNF   c1

3 3045 00033 5303

Presented to

_____

By _____

Date _____

God Speaks to a King

Bible Stories in Rhythm and Rhyme

Written by **Sheri Dunham Haan**

Illustrated by **Dan Hochstatter**

j 220. 950
HAA

Text copyright 1974 by Baker Book House Company
Used with permission.
ISBN: 0-8010-4357-3

© 1991 Educational Publishing Concepts, Inc., Wheaton IL 60187
All rights reserved. Except for brief excerpts for review purposes, no part of
this book may be reproduced or used in any form without written permission from the publisher.

Exclusive distribution by Baker Book House, Grand Rapids, Michigan

8.95

Contents

921983

Preface

Although rhythm and stories both date back almost farther in history than we can trace, very few such stories are based on the Bible. And even fewer have been written down for young children to enjoy.

Nursery age children will probably enjoy the stories most by hearing them read. Soon children begin clapping hands or tapping feet while they listen to the strong cadence. Older children will want to do more complicated clapping rhythms. A family with young children can use these stories effectively as devotions.

Read these stories at a pace that is comfortable for you. As you become more familiar with them, you and your child will enjoy a quick, lively pace. Read a line and have your child chant it back to you. Use the stories as a happy, natural way to reinforce Bible truths.

God Speaks to a King

—Selected passages from Exodus 7–12

Moses and Aaron stood firm by the throne

Giving God's orders to Pharaoh alone:

"You MUST let the Israelites go!"

This made the king very angry and mad,

These were the only slaves that he had.

In no way would he let them go!

God turned all the rivers and water to blood,

The land truly stunk with the smelly red mud

But Pharaoh would not let them go!

Then frogs simply covered the land

And lice nibbled on cattle and man,

Still Pharaoh would not let them go!

Next came the sores,
　　　　they were large, tender boils.
Then golfballs of ice
　　　　just pounded the soil,
But Pharaoh did not let them go!

Great grasshoppers gobbled
        the greens of the land,
Then darkness set in—
        you could not see your hand.
Yet, Pharaoh would not let them go!

And finally the last plague
       that made people weep,
Many Egyptian sons
       died in their sleep.
Will this make the king let them go?

When Pharaoh knew that his own son had died,

Meekly and sadly he called out and cried,

"Moses, please take them! Yes! Go!"

The Israelites started packing their things

Taking their masters' gold bracelets and rings.

At last they were free and could go!

At last they were free! They could go!

God's Winning Plan
—Judges 7:1-9, 16-22

God spoke to his general,
His name was Gideon,
"Prepare to meet in battle
All the men of Midian."

"Now you will win the battle
But you'll win it by my might.
Send every single soldier home
Who is afraid to fight."

More than half of Gideon's men
Left for home that day.
Yet still the army was too large
To fight the war God's way.

Gideon followed God's next plan
To watch how each man drank.
He brought them to the river,
Most men knelt along the bank.

Three hundred men bent over
Taking water in their hands.
These were the few God wanted
To fight his winning plan.

With pitchers, lamps,
and horns they left.
They took no guns or swords.
And when they neared
the camp they cried,
"For Gideon and the Lord!"

921983

The enemy was really scared!
Some quickly ran to hide,
The others fought among themselves—
The winner was God's side!
Yes!
The winner was God's side!

God Is God Alone
—1 Kings 18

Elijah called King Ahab
And all the priests of Baal,
He called them to the mountain
To see God's plan unveil.

Loud and clear Elijah called,
"We're gathered here today
To find at last whose god is real,
And whose god to obey."

"Two altars you and I will build.
We'll need some wood and stone;
Whichever god will send down fire
Is God and God alone!"

Baal's prophets built their altar
Then danced around and cried,
"Dear Baal, you must send fire!"
But Baal gave no reply.

"I think your Baal is sleeping,"
Elijah teased and smiled;
"Or maybe he's out walking
For just a little while."

Elijah built his altar,

He soaked it through and through;

And then Elijah prayed out loud,

"Dear Father, show us you!"

Then fire flashed from heaven
It burned the wood and stone!
And everyone who saw it cried,
"God is God alone!"
   "Yes!"
      "God is God alone!"

A Very Scary Storm
—*Matthew 8:23-27*

Jesus climbed into a boat
One very busy day,
So many folks had followed him—
He hoped to get away.

Jesus was so tired,

He sat and propped his feet.

It wasn't very long before

The Lord was fast asleep.

And then the sky turned greenish black,
A wind began to blow.
Waves pounded hard against the boat
They tipped it to and fro.

The frightened friends of Jesus
Cried out in pleading calls,
"Jesus, Master, save us!
The storm will drown us all!"

Jesus quickly wakened.

He was sad that they had called.

His dearest friends did not believe

That he was Lord of ALL!

Then Jesus turned and faced the storm.

He called out, "Peace, be still!"

The winds and waves were gone at once!

They did the Master's will.

Surprise at Sunrise

—Mark 16:1-8

The three ladies hurried
To visit the tomb,
Their hearts were just filled
With sadness and gloom!

But as they arrived

They were shocked and surprised.

That large heavy stone

Had been rolled to one side!

They stepped to the door
Not believing their eyes!
An angel was speaking,
"Now, don't be surprised."

"You've come to see Jesus,
But he isn't here.
He's come back to life,
You need have no fear!"

"Now go back to town
And tell all your friends
That Jesus is living—
You'll see him again!"

The three ladies turned
And hurried away;
Jesus, their Savior—
Alive on this day!

A Very Changed Man
—Acts 9:1-9, 18-19

Paul left on his journey
With chains in both his hands,
He hunted hated Christians
Through his entire land.

As he neared Damascus
There was a dazzling light;
Blinded Paul fell on his knees,
He knew he'd lost his sight.

And then a voice from heaven
Called out so loud and clear,
"Paul, why do you hurt me
And all my people here?"

Paul heard this person speaking
As he lay there on the ground,
But he and his companions
Were the only ones around.

Paul cried out, "Who's speaking?
Who blinded me this way?"
The voice called back, "It's Jesus,
Your life will change today."

Paul went to the city,
And when three days had passed
God opened up his eyes again
So he could see at last!

Stories I liked best of all